DESIGN RESOURCE SERIES

# STREAMLINE

## MARC ARCENEAUX

ART AND DESIGN OF THE FORTIES

TROUBADOR PRESS
SAN FRANCISCO

To Susan

### Troubador DESIGN RESOURCE Series

The DESIGN RESOURCE Series provides graphic references and design motifs with photographs, illustrations, and patterns ready to use. The illustrations in this book may be reproduced on any non-commercial project for home or classroom free and without special permission. Include a credit line indicating the book title and publisher. Write the publisher for permission to make more extensive use of the materials in the book or for commercial purposes. The republication of this book in whole or in part beyond the specifications above is prohibited.

Library of Congress Cataloging in Publication Data

Arceneaux, Marc, 1947-
    Streamline: art & design of the forties.

    (The Design resource series)
    1. Design, Industrial — United States — History.
2. Design — United States — History.  I. Title.
TS23.A7            745.2'0973            75-37664
ISBN 0-912300-63-9

DESIGNED BY: MARC ARCENEAUX
GRAPHICS: MARC ARCENEAUX, GUY ARCENEAUX, AND TIMOTHY GAUSS
TEXT: PETER ROSE, MARC ARCENEAUX, AND DAVID HARRISON III
GRAPHIC ASSISTANCE: CIRCUS LITHO, SAN FRANCISCO, CALIFORNIA
TYPESET: LIBRA ARTS, SAN FRANCISCO, CALIFORNIA
RESEARCH ASSISTANCE: SEAN DONAHUE

AN ACE◇ART BOOK DESIGN

# CONTENTS

4.  INTRODUCTION

6.  CULTURE

19.  ARCHITECTURE

30.  TRANSPORTATION

43.  FUTURE

**DESIGN PLATE INFORMATION**
The designated design pages found throughout this book are ideally suited for all manner of graphic reproduction and craft applications. The design plates are representative of the images associated with the Streamline era.

The Nazi blitzkrieg swept mercilessly across Europe, and the menace posed by Japanese Imperialism in the Pacific grew more ominous with each passing day. Like it or not, America in the early forties was a country mobilized by multilateral threat to its very existence.

Uncle Sam's inevitable entry into this cataclysmic global conflict brought with it an overwhelming commitment to patriotic duty and victory. The Selective Training and Service Bill — the draft — had been passed in 1940, but after Pearl Harbor most of the country's able-bodied young men were more than willing to join in the fight to make the world safe for democracy. The rest of the population contributed to the war effort in other ways. They worked day and night in war plants, bought war bonds, tended their victory gardens, endured tedious food and fuel rations, recycled their scrap metals, and even saved waste paper for packing cartons.

The cumulative effect of these sacrifices over a few years surprised America. By 1943, U.S. Steel production was estimated at 90,000,000 tons per year, five full-blown ocean-going vessels were launched every 24 hours and the railroads covered an incredible 412,000,000,000 freight ton miles. After lingering in the throes of depression at the outset of the war, America emerged from it in the midst of a boom.

The task of winning the war seemed to relegate the country's cultural and artistic life to a subsidiary position. Historical hindsight indicates that the war actually helped further the development of streamline design in two significant ways. It stimulated progress in aerodynamics and provided an influx of refugee artists from Europe.

In streamlining an object, the entire consideration is to minimize the resistance to a flow of air or water over its contours, increasing the rate of speed while maintaining or reducing the energy requirements.

This efficiency of form became paramount during the war years as aeronautics enabled our planes to attain air speeds and altitudes of which we had only dreamed a few years before. Trains, ships, boats, and automobiles benefited from streamlining.

In the thirties, the U.S. government, in an unprecedented legislative move, had agreed to subsidize American artists and authors by commissioning works of art for government projects. The W.P.A. (Works Progress Administration) supported many artists during the hard depression years. I. Rice Pereira, Ben Shahn, Jack Levine, Stuart Davis, and Jackson Pollock received sponsorship and this act of bureaucratic friendliness encouraged and generally sustained the American art com-

# INTRODUCTION

munity, creating a cordial and receptive atmosphere for artists fleeing the oppressive nationalistic policies of wartime Europe.

The Bauhaus was the most important school of modern design in Europe. Noted for the clean functional lines of streamline architecture and investigative abstract quality of its art and sculpture, the school was closed by Hitler who considered its teachings decadent and un-German.

Laszlo Moholy-Nagy, Josef Albers, Mies Van De Rohe, and Walter Gropius — these Bauhaus artists and many others from Europe immigrated to the United States. New York replaced Paris as the center of the avant garde.

The fabric of life itself had changed drastically in less than a decade, from bi-planes, at the outset of the war, to jets, rockets, and atomic power in a scant five years.

A public, long fed daily doses of Buck Rogers, Flash Gordon, and Superman, began to see that space travel, moon landings, and space stations were to be realities in its lifetime.

Streamlining represented an uncomplicated future world, no shadows unaccounted for, every step delineated. Americans looked toward tomorrow with unbridled optimism.

# CULTURE

# FINE ARTS

**Walter Gropius**

**Walter Gropius**

**Laszlo Moholy-Nagy**

**Josef Albers**

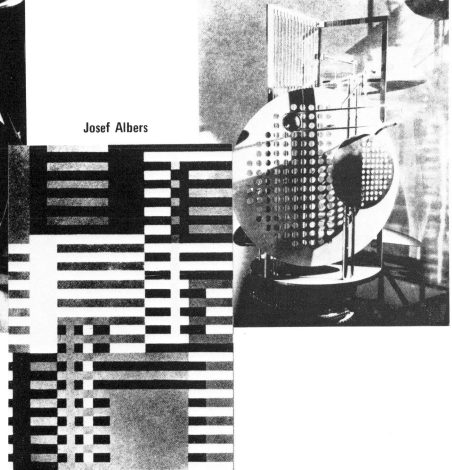

8

# WOMEN'S FASHIONS

Dictated by war shortages instead of Paris, the wide-shouldered geometric inspired styles of the early forties were austere, simple of line and subdued in color.

After 1945, much of the synthetics developed for military uses became extensively featured in fashions. Miracle fabrics offered a variety of colors and textures heretofore unknown. Rayon and nylon joined cotton and wool as desirable clothing materials.

Asymmetrical, duo-tone streamline designs and the fast-rising casual California look assured America a place of importance in the fashion world by 1949.

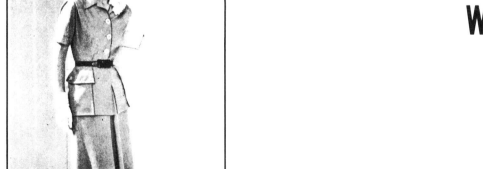

DESIGN PLATE 1

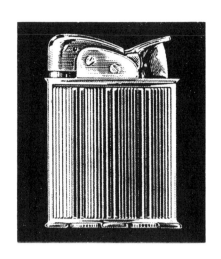

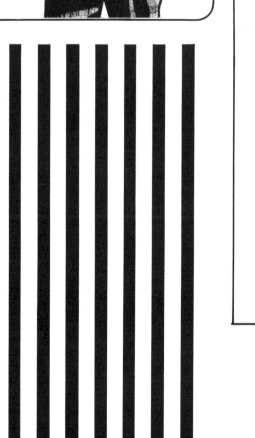

STREAM-LINED
SMOKING PIPE

MADE OF A
PACIFIC
FABRIC

# MEN'S FASHIONS

Spanning the decade, men's fashions went from the military uniform to aloha print shirts and white and black shoes, a casual look popularized by president Harry Truman.

Somberly colored double-breasted suits with heavily padded shoulders were highlighted by a streamline-patterned tie, which was virtually the only bastion of male individuality still tolerated in the workaday business costume.

Zippers and snaps (initially referred to as grippers) made their commercial appearance, beginning a trend toward sleekness and practical comfort.

1948 Portable radio

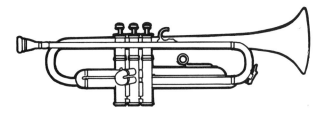

# MUSIC

Swinging into the forties, big bands carried the message to radio listeners across the continent. "Praise The Lord and Pass The Ammunition," a song written by Frank Loesser to commemorate a Navy chaplain's immortal courageous words, typified the patriotic mood of Tin Pan Alley. Glenn Miller and his band travelled extensively, boosting soldiers' morale overseas.

Meanwhile, back home, a new phenomenon was taking place. He was called "The Voice," and bobby-soxers nationwide were swooning for Frank Sinatra.

The Modernaires' smoothness of harmony, the slick delivery of Dick Haymes and Joe Stafford, Mel Torme's flawless, straight-line, round-toned singing, and the shining drive of Woody Herman and Charlie Barnett with "Skyliner," all reflected the brilliance of the streamline era.

Design plate 2 is a rendering of a Wurlitzer juke box.

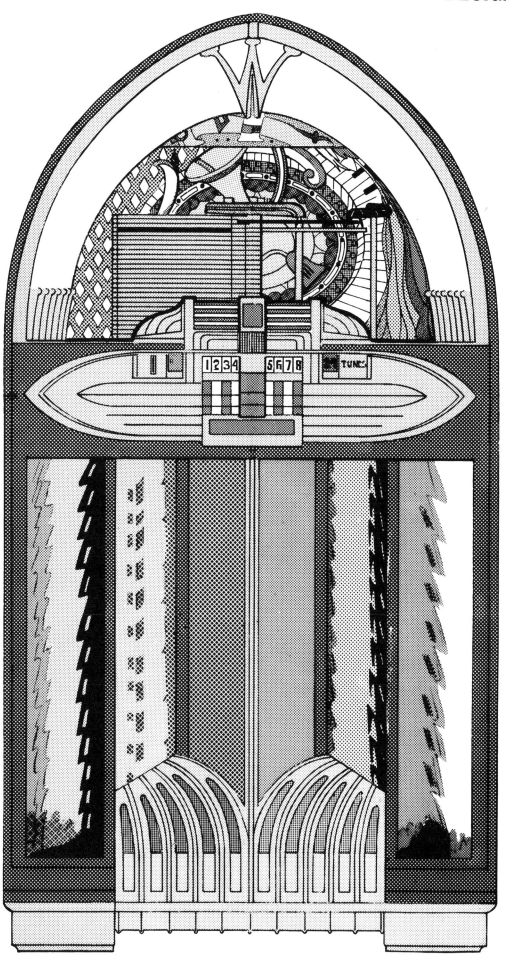

GREAT CONTRIBUTIONS
TO GOOD TASTE

# ADVERTISING ART

Advertising art in the forties, when not patriotic in nature, tended to depict idealized people and highly streamlined landscapes. Lettering was bold block style and colors were vibrant and pure with much emphasis on the primaries.

A B C
D E F
! G H I
J K L

M N O
P Q R
S T U
V W X

Y Z & 2 3 4 5 6 7 8 9 ?

# ARCHITECTURE

# Hurricane House Turns with Wind

## WEATHER-VANE DWELLING DESIGNED FOR BOTH SAFETY AND COMFORT

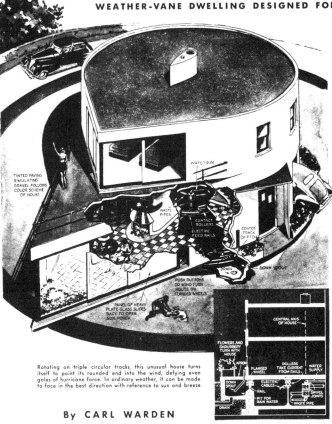

TINTED PAVING SIMULATING GRAVEL, FOLLOWS COLOR SCHEME OF HOUSE

WATER PIPE

WASTE PIPES

CONTACT ROLLERS

ELECTRIC FEED RAILS

CENTER TRACK (31 FT. DIA.)

DRAIN

DOWN SPOUT

PUSH BUTTONS OR WIND TURN HOUSE ON FLANGED WHEELS

PANEL OF HEAVY PLATE GLASS SLIDES BACK TO OPEN SUN PORCH

Rotating on triple circular tracks, this unusual house turns itself to point its rounded end into the wind, defying even gales of hurricane force. In ordinary weather, it can be made to face in the best direction with reference to sun and breeze

**By CARL WARDEN**

CENTRAL AXIS OF HOUSE

FLOWERS AND SHRUBBERY TURN WITH HOUSE

APRON

ROLLERS TAKE CURRENT FROM RAILS

WATER SUPPLY

DOWN SPOUT

FLANGED WHEEL

ELECTRIC CABLES

RAIL

PIT FOR RAIN WATER

SWIVEL JOINTS

DRAIN

WASTE PIPE

WHEN raging storms whip across the land, accompanied by violent gales that uproot trees, tear the roofs from houses, and turn a trim countryside into a scene of desolation, there could probably be no safer refuge than the interior of a novel hurricane house designed by Edwin A. Koch, New York City architect. Streamline in the form of a mammoth teardrop, this amazing dwelling would revolve automatically to face into the oncoming storm, meeting it like the wing of an airplane and passing it smoothly around its curving sides toward its pointed tip.

Although planned for areas subject to periodic winds of gale force, the unique home has other unusual features that adapt it to luxurious living in any climate. Constructed of light steel channels and I-beam sections

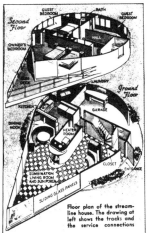

Second Floor

GUEST BEDROOM

BATH

GUEST BEDROOM

OWNER'S BEDROOM

HALL

DECK

LAUNDRY

Ground Floor

KITCHEN

GARAGE

DINING ROOM

HEATER ROOM

COMBINATION LIVING ROOM AND SUN PORCH

CLOSET

ENTRANCE

SLIDING GLASS PANELS

Floor plan of the streamline house. The drawing at left shows the tracks and the service connections

bolted together, the house has insulated walls faced on the exterior with semiflexible waterproof plywood. The entire structure rests on flanged wheels similar in construction to those found on a highway or railroad drawbridge. These run on three separate circular tracks: an inner track twelve feet in diameter, a second, placed just below the exterior walls, measuring thirty-one feet in diameter, and an outside, sixty-eight foot track for a wheel located at the pointed tip of the dwelling and cleverly concealed by an indoor living-room flower-bed.

A cantilevered floor covered with boiler plate extends beyond the outside walls for a distance of four feet to prevent driving rains from beating into the pit below the house, and to form an apron for the garage, a platform for the entrance doorways, and a ledge for flower boxes. Electricity enters the building through the inner track, while the water-supply and sewage pipes come in underground at the axis on which the house turns, swivel joints being provided to connect the stationary exterior pipes with those which are attached to the dwelling.

Inside the house, the first floor provides an entrance hall, a triangular living room with a built-in dining section on one side and a built-in library nook on the other, a kitchen, laundry, heater room, and a garage having space for a workbench and a trapdoor that provides access to the piping, wiring, and track mechanisms in the foundation pit below. Upstairs there are three large bedrooms, two baths, and a spacious open sun deck. Garage doors, and most of the broad expanse of glass windows, slide into the walls.

Merely by selecting the desired push button on a central control board, the entire house may be rotated to face rooms toward or away from the sun or to point bedroom windows toward a cooling breeze.

## Streamlined city hall building with an airport on its roof.

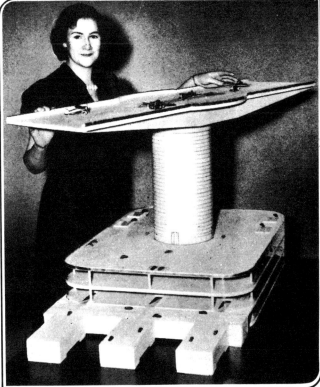

By designing and producing examples of modernistic
furniture, buildings and homes, the futurist de-
signers of 1917, Corbusier in the twenties, and the
Bauhaus school of design in the thirties all contributed to the acceptance of streamline.

The streamlining of man's environment was
widespread by 1940. Rounded corners inspired by
aerodynamics found their way into and on buildings
of every description. Gas stations, skyscrapers and
news-stands received the streamline treatment.

Every facet of consumer hardward on the
market was slicked down, smoothed over and
modernized. Many of these forties appliances are
still sold today with no design change.

# It's Brand New!

# GREATEST *Magic Chef* YET!

automatic — beautifully streamlined and so efficient

Man's industrial revolution, begun in the last century, culminated in the late twenties with efficient machines that were more advanced than their archaic physical forms.

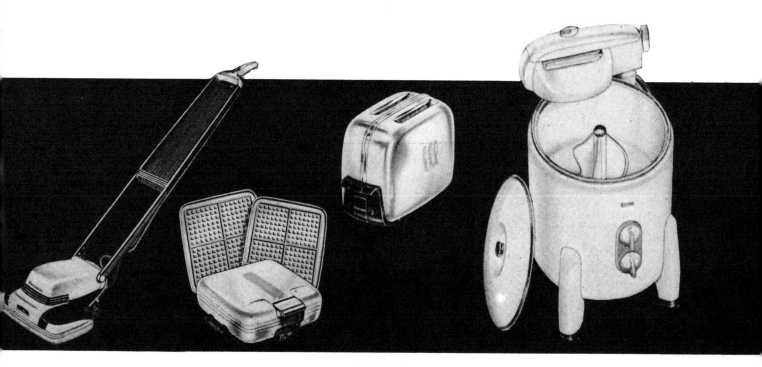

Light and music emanate from this table lamp, the base contains a hidden radio.

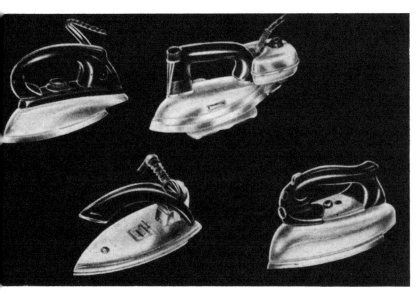

In pursuing the dream of a mechanized society, the machine had surpassed its creators' intentions. A 1927 Chrysler was more aerodynamic driving backwards because it was designed in the same manner as a horse drawn carriage. There was no consideration for the sophisticated engine which powered it, the chassis' high degree of evolvement, or the aerodynamics of streamlining.

When the machinery finally lost its novelty, the ungainly contours and exposed gearing of both vehicles and appliances were considered unacceptable.

This realization prompted a total redesign of everything from automobiles to electric mouse traps during the thirties, and by the 1940's streamline design was an integral part of life in the United States.

Using a good grade of ¾ inch lumber, cut out two sets of the pattern shapes presented here and construct a unique streamlined pair of bookends. The parts may be glued, nailed, or screwed together. After fine sanding paint with gloss black enamel.

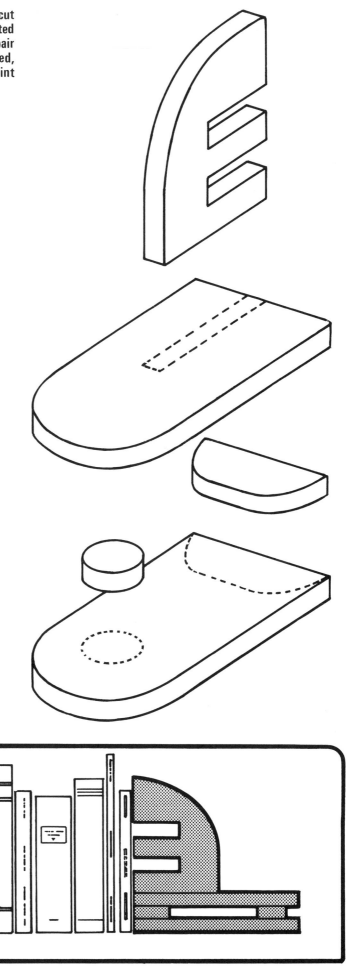

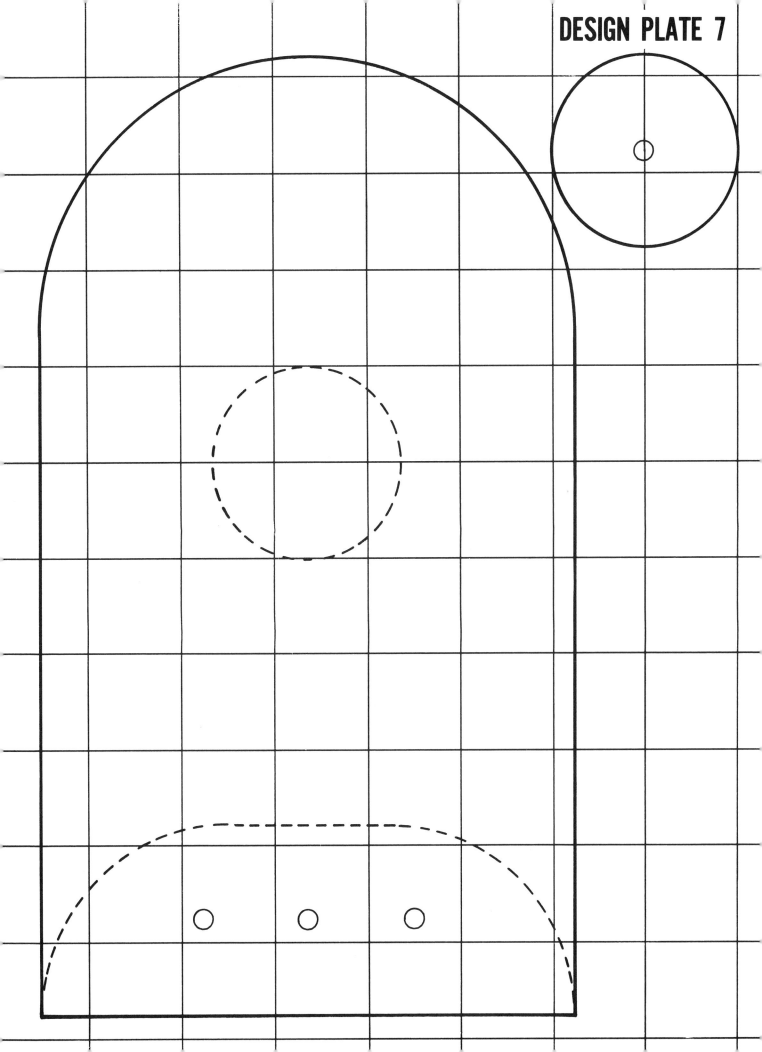

DESIGN PLATE 7

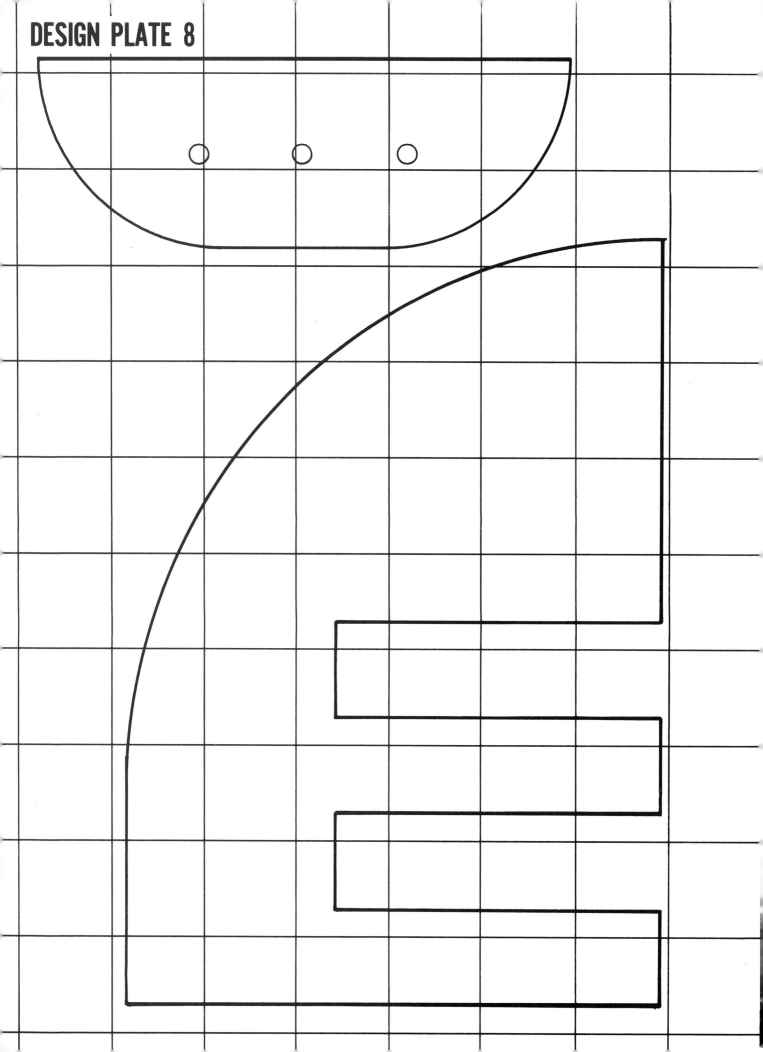

DESIGN PLATE 8

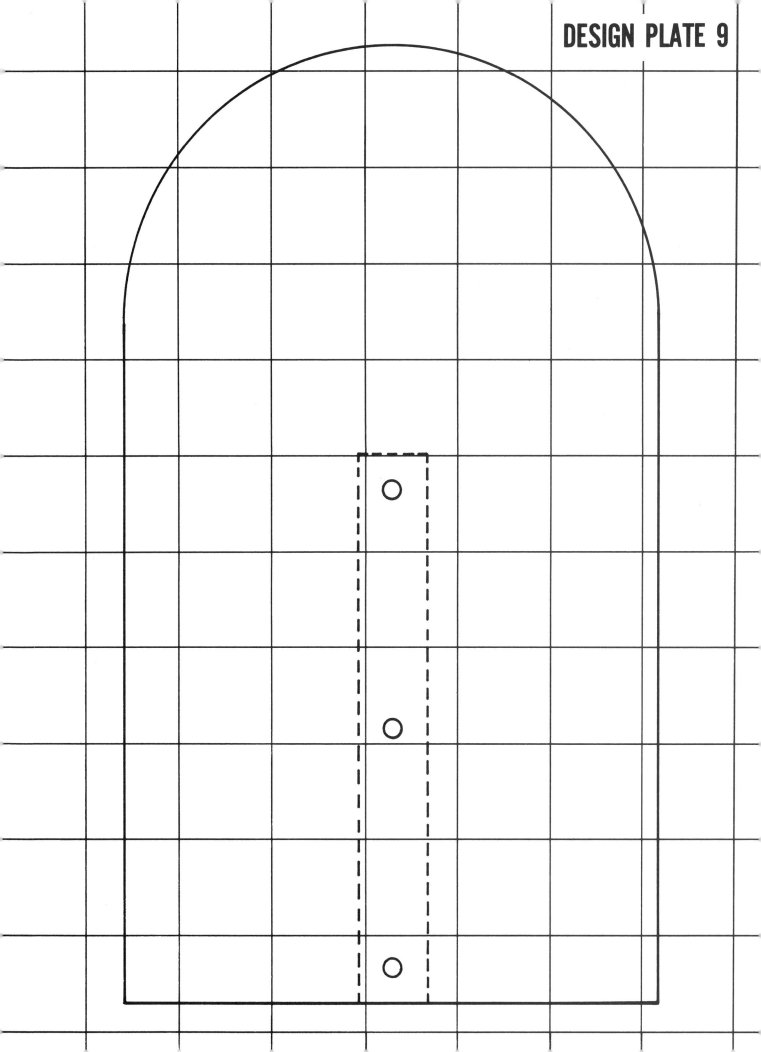

DESIGN PLATE 9

# TRANSPORTATION

There's something about a new Studebaker
that gets people really excited

**1942**

**1947**

We created the machine; now the machine would dictate and shape our aesthetic needs.

Gone was the hand crafted, one-completed-unit-at-a-time method of production. Now assembly lines speedily manufactured consumer goods, which were specifically designed for this new production technique.

The essence of Streamline is best defined as a balanced combination of the following characteristics: fluted or ribbed panels surrounding the lower portion of an object; detailing such as flush mounted stainless steel windows, chromium ringed portholes, daring expanses and placement of glass; and a totally controlled, machine-like quality unblemished by man's idiosyncratic carvings and embellishments.

**195?**

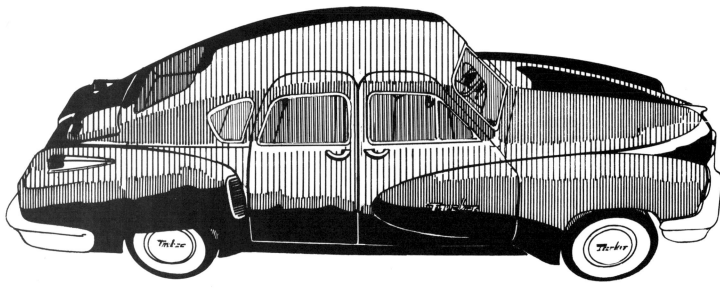

# 1948
# TUCKER

Beechcrafts' 1946 Plainsman.

An Alex Termulis streamline design.

Tremulis' 1941 Chrysler Thunderbolt.

A P-38 (see pg. 42) inspired design.

"... someday the future may catch up with the past," Alex Tremulis, designer of the rear engined 1948 Tucker safety car.

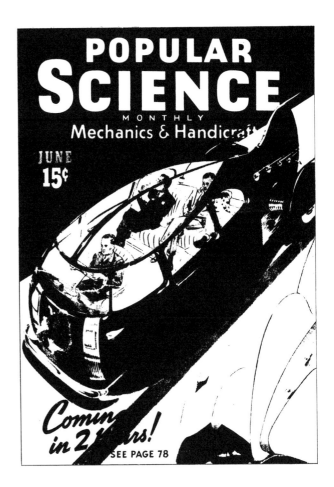

An optimistic Popular Science magazine cover from 1940, its headline promising modern streamline automobiles in two years.

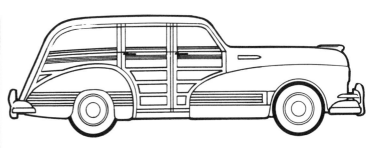

1946 Pontiac station wagon

33

A.

A. Resembling a whale, this sixteen-foot racing boat features a glass enclosed cockpit.

B. The speedy motorcycle car is guided by a steering wheel and rides on two wheels.

C. Greyhound Corporation's Scenicruiser offered an observation lounge and full washroom facilities for all passengers.

D. An ultra modern roadster, designed by comedian Ralph Cook, was capable of 96 m.p.h. speeds, yet averaged gas mileage of 29 miles per gallon.

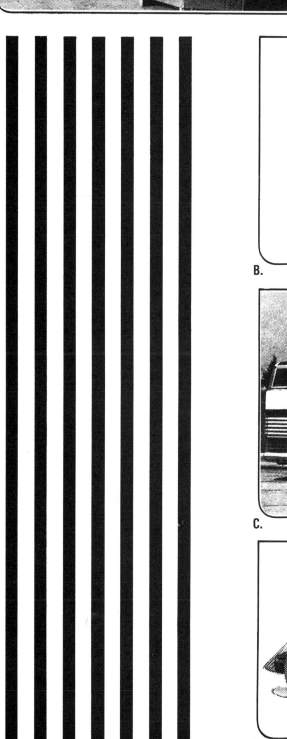

B.

C.

D.

A. This luxurious trailer combines home and office for a New York advertising man. Equipped with a 1,000-watt radio transmitter, observation windows and accommodations for six.

B. Constructed in Hollywood, California, this auto is fully streamlined except for its wheels.

C. Resplendent with bullet-shaped headlight, streamlined tank and chain guard, this Columbia bicycle was the ultimate for many forties youngsters.

D. This streamline yacht appears to be a submarine at first glance.

A.

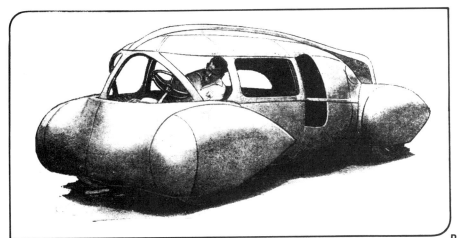

B.

C.

D.

35

A.

B.

C.

A. One of the famed Hiawatha locomotives sparkles as it is prepared for an outbound trip.

B. General Electric's experimental turbine locomotive.

C. Built in 1948, a diesel-electric car of this type could do 75 m.p.h.

Reaching a zenith in the early forties, railroads linked every metropolis, town, and hamlet with shining rails of steel for glistening crack streamliners.

The train, with it's mammoth proportions and power, sheathed in bright stainless steel and streamlined to perfection, became the prevalent design influence through the forties.

Train interior designs by Raymond Lowey.

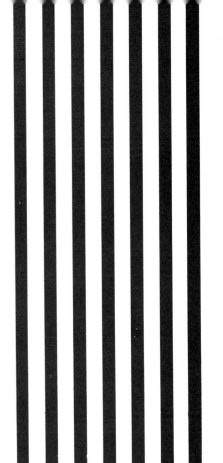

CHICAGO·MILWAUKEE·ST. PAUL·MINNEAPOLIS

CHICAGO
MILWAUKEE
ST PAUL
AND PACIFIC

*Hiawatha*

NOTHING FASTER
ON RAILS

A luggage label from the Streamline era.

# FLIGHT FOR EVERYONE

The great advance in aeronautical technology made during the 1940s manifested itself in the streamliners of the sky.

The American public was wooed with massive advertising campaigns. Airlines promised overnight flights with berths and radar navigation. They guaranteed swift, silent engines to whisk you and your loved ones to that home cooked Thanksgiving dinner at Grandma's — out of state and back again in less time than an auto would take one way.

The subsequent increase in airplane flights was a boon to the travel industry and Americans were now the most mobile people on earth.

Airlines save you time . . .

offer luxury travel and . . .

bring families closer together.

# FUTURE

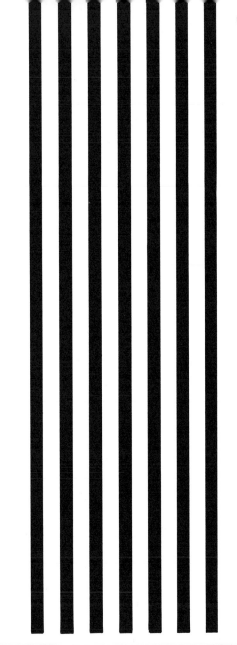

After the austerity of the war years, Americans looked forward to an unprecedented boom in consumer goods and services. All plans for the future were based on the stupendous growth rate of production during the early forties and, thus, were grossly exaggerated. It was predicted that by the end of the decade each family would have a private plane in addition to the family car; that helicopters and fast mini-planes would provide urban mass transit; and that pre-fabricated houses would be available to everyone at low cost, including mansions for $5,000 and palaces for $10,000. Other predictions for the future were accurate in substance through they have become realities only recently. Wall-size TV, all-electric kitchens, supersonic jetliners and solar heat — in the last half of the 1940s all were thought to be just over the horizon in that rush of post-war optimism.

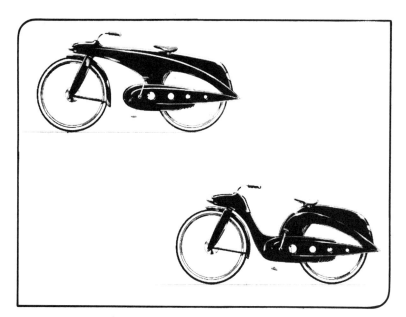

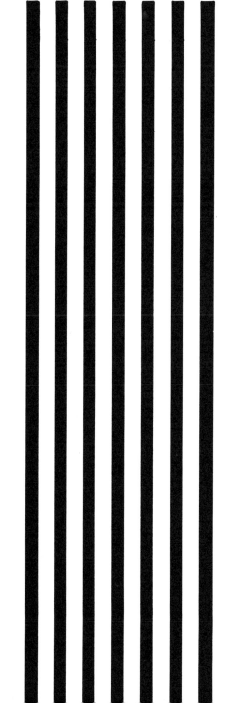

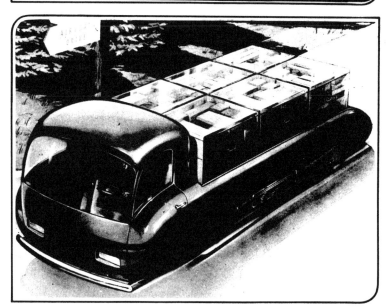

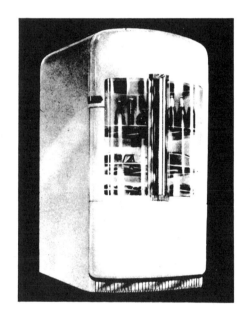

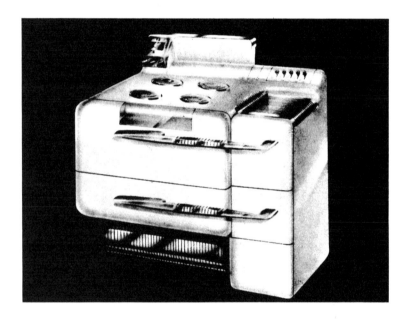

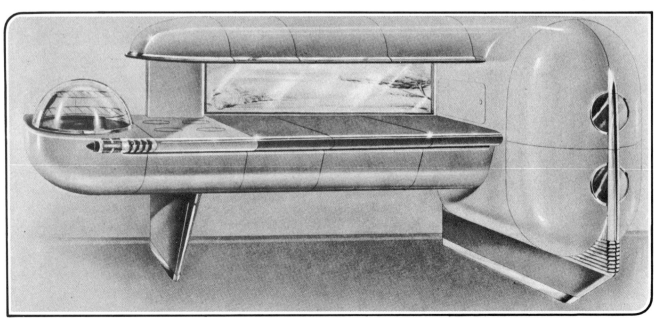

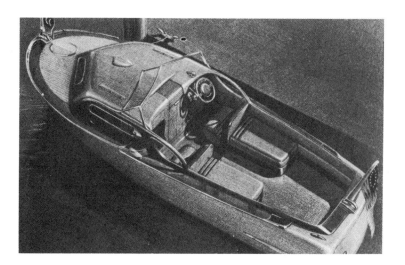

Automobile and train design influences are evident in these renderings of streamlined pleasure craft.

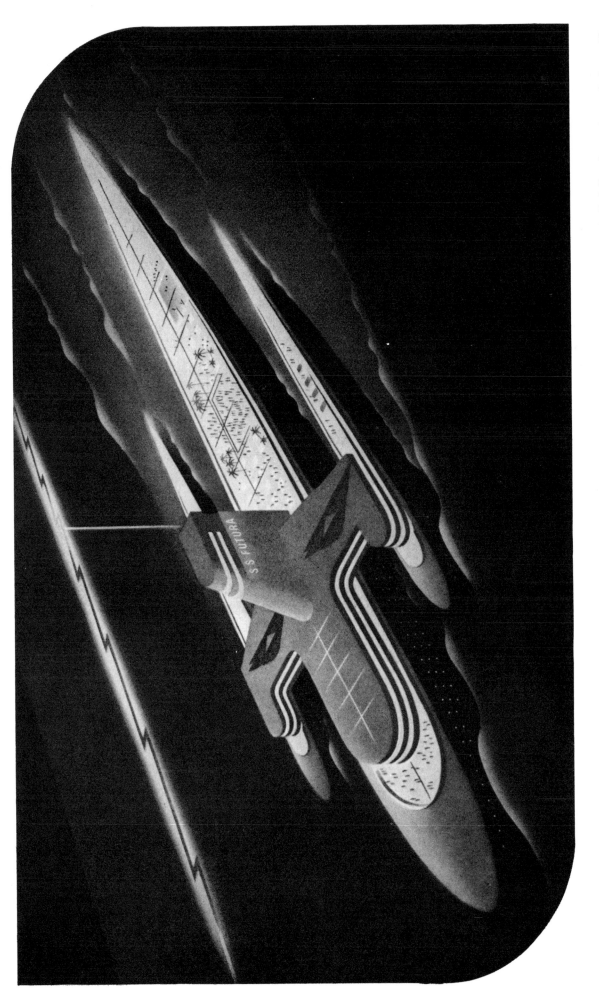

Deriving its power from a radio beam, this triple-hulled floating palace of dream-like luxury will span the oceans carrying 5,000 passengers at unbelievable speed — steadied by the pontoon design. Social life will center in the main streamliner, with swimming pool, dance floors, promenades and spacious salons. Sleeping quarters will be in the smaller ships. Planes will take off from the hangar deck for foreign capitals as the liner approaches shore.